THE PRIMACY OF DRAWING

An Artist's View

EXHIBITION TOUR

Bristol Museum and Art Gallery, 21 September – 3 November 1991

City Museum and Art Gallery, Stoke on Trent, 9 November – 5 January 1992

Graves Art Gallery, Sheffield, 11 January – 23 February 1992

A National Touring Exhibition from the South Bank Centre
Exhibition organised by Roger Malbert
assisted by Julia Coates
Education Officer Helen Luckett
Catalogue designed by Crispin Rose-Innes Ltd
Printed in England by Dot for Dot Ltd
© The South Bank Centre 1991
ISBN 1 85332 078 1
A full list of Arts Council and South Bank Centre publications may be obtained from:
Art Publications, South Bank Centre, Royal Festival Hall, London SE1 8XX

Cover:
1 ALBRECHT DÜRER (1471-1528) *Head of the Dead Christ,*
Trustees of the British Museum

THE PRIMACY OF
DRAWING

An Artist's View

Deanna Petherbridge

A NATIONAL TOURING EXHIBITION FROM
THE SOUTH BANK CENTRE 1991

LENDERS TO THE EXHIBITION

Birmingham City Museums and Art Gallery 100, 111, 120

Cambridge, The Syndics of the Fitzwilliam Museum 1, 2, 7, 10, 19, 30, 31, 32, 81, 85, 86, 98, 105, 114, 115, 116, 117, 119, 122, 131, 138, 142

Cambridge, Kettle's Yard, University of Cambridge 48

Ivan Florence 25

Howard Hodgkin 73, 107

Holkham Hall, Viscount Coke and the Trustees of the Holkham Estate 17, 23, 24, 118

Libbie Howie and John Pillar Fine Art 87

Leeds City Art Galleries 11, 26 27, 39, 51, 54, 129

Leicestershire Museums, Arts and Records Service 77

London, British Architectural Library Drawings Collection/Royal Institute of British Architects 47, 70, 84, 139

London, Trustees of the British Museum 3, 4, 6, 18, 21, 22, 33, 34, 35, 36, 37, 44, 45, 46, 55, 58, 60, 62, 63, 64, 65, 67, 68, 75, 94, 104, 126, 132, 133, 134

London, Courtauld Institute Galleries (Witt Collection) 12, 13, 16, 95, 103

London, The Trustees of the Imperial War Museum 8, 92, 128

London, Tate Gallery 5, 57, 59, 78, 93, 106, 112

London, The Board of Trustees of the Victoria & Albert Museum 43, 61, 89, 109, 110, 123, 136

Manchester City Art Galleries 82

Manchester, Whitworth Art Gallery, University of Manchester 14, 28, 41, 42, 96, 125, 141

Oxford, The Visitors of the Ashmolean Museum 15, 38, 69, 99, 102, 121, 140, 143, 144

Oxford, The Governing Body, Christ Church 20, 29, 52, 56, 91, 97, 113, 127, 130, 135, 137

Paula Rego 108

Robert and Lisa Sainsbury Collection, University of East Anglia 53, 90, 124

Karsten Schubert Ltd 9

Sheffield City Art Galleries 40, 74, 79, 83

Mr and Mrs Dennis Wiseman 66, 72, 76

Private Collections 49, 50, 71, 80, 88, 101

FOREWORD

This publication marks the first of a series of South Bank Centre exhibitions selected by artists and writers with a particular interest in drawing. Deanna Petherbridge is both an accomplished draughts-woman and an eloquent exponent of the art of drawing; her insights bring a fresh perspective to a subject which is rarely dealt with in print in other than specialist terms, of technique or historical scholarship.

Drawing is at the heart of the visual arts. It is, quite literally, where most artists begin. Yet for the museum collection, works on paper present particular problems. Their vulnerability to the effects of exposure to light means that they cannot be placed on permanent display. The opportunity to see a wide range of drawings of quality outside the framework of monographic or historical survey exhibitions is therefore rare. We are especially grateful to the major museums for responding so generously to this project, allowing us to include many Old Master drawings of the highest order. Ironically, one effect of their exceptional generosity has been to limit the contemporary drawings to fewer than the selector had originally intended.

Our thanks are due firstly to Deanna Petherbridge for the enthusiasm and conviction with which she has undertaken this project. The result is testimony to the extent of her research and the depth of her appreciation of the subject. We are indebted to all the lenders, and to the following, who have given valuable assistance and advice: David Alston, Philippa Alden, Hugh Belsey, Fiona J.M. Brown, Frances Carey, Terry Friedman, Antony Griffiths, Howard Hodgkin, Sarah Hyde, David Penn, Frederick C. Jolly, Sandra Martin, Jane McAusland, Claire Messenger, Jennifer Ramkalawon, Janice Reading, Bryan Robertson, Martin Royalton-Kisch, David Scrase, Tessa Sidey, Juliet Steyn, Nicholas Turner, Angela Weight, Catherine Whistler, T.H. Wilson, Lucy Whitaker and Jenny Wood.

Joanna Drew
Director,
Hayward and Regional Exhibitions

Roger Malbert
Exhibition Organiser

2 THOMAS VAUGHAN *Study in Sciagraphy* 1857, British Architectural Library Drawings Collection, Royal Institute of British Architects

INTRODUCTION

This exhibition is based on the notion of the primal nature of drawing, its universality and economy of means, its expressive intensity, its ability to reveal process and autograph. Drawing is the primal means of symbolic communication, which predates and embraces writing and functions as a tool of conceptualisation parallel with language. It is the artistic medium which is least interrupted by technical considerations and therefore the chosen means for the initial formulation of visual ideas and the transfer or appropriation of visual culture. Drawing lacks materiality in comparison with painting. This together with its ubiquity and functionality is probably why, outside of the estimation of 'master drawings', the medium is generally undervalued. Though not by artists.

I was invited to select this exhibition because I have done nothing but draw for years. I'd thought about drawing, and written about it in relation to my own practice, but this was the first time I had really looked systematically and thought about the subject in general. Looking at drawings in museum cabinets, exhibitions and studios was wonderfully pleasurable. Writing this catalogue has been extremely difficult. Perhaps because of my simultaneous need and hesitancy to legitimise instinctive assumptions, perhaps because the whole subject of drawing is too close to the bone. I wanted to say more than 'I've chosen such and such a work because I like it', and have found myself theorising and speculating at some length. Having been constantly amazed and delighted by correspondences between drawings from different times and different cultures, I have found myself challenging some of the narratives of art history.

One regret is that an exhibition cannot convey the pleasures that come from handling a drawing. That intimacy, that conversation with the work, cannot be replicated by drawings distanced behind glass and hung vertically on walls. Like most people, until I started my researches, I had assumed that museum drawing cabinets were fearful halls of entombment, open only to the legitimate scholars who could ask the right questions to unlock the drawers. On the contrary, I found them friendly places – in particular the Prints and Drawings Room of the British Museum – where one can breathe over drawings and commune with them, or turn the pages of sketchbooks in casual serendipity. The unfolding and serial nature of drawing is best enjoyed in a portfolio or sketchbook, but opening just one page of a book in a glass case is so unsatisfactory, that I chose not to include any in the exhibition.

Another regret is that I have included so few drawings by women. I discovered that there are very few Old Mistresses in museums,

3 ANGELICA KAUFFMAN (1740–1807) *The Letter: Half Length Figure Seated at a Table*, Trustees of the British Museum

although Britain has a magnificent resource of Old Master drawings, on a par with France and Italy. (Public collections here are also singularly lacking in foreign 20th century drawings.) I couldn't help laughing, ruefully, over my anguish over Anguissola. I had been poring over Van Dyck's Italian sketchbook, and in time came to his notes of his visit to Palermo and his moving sketch of the aged Sofonisba Anguissola to whom he went to pay homage. To my delight I discovered a drawing attributed to her in the collection only to be told, when I asked to borrow it, that it had been re-attributed to some minor male artist! Women's drawings were regularly copied in the compilation copy-books of 'master' drawings of the 17th and 18th centuries, which indicates that they were not undervalued then. Hopefully many drawings will be re-attributed to women and recouped for enjoyment in the future.

I had also hoped to include more drawings from other than European cultures in the exhibition, but this has not proved possible, except for a few Indian and Japanese drawings. The section on drawings which are close to geometry would have benefited from miniatures exploring Islamic geometric design if I could have found monochromatic examples; the category *The Sinuous Line* would have been enriched by examples of Persian calligraphic drawing styles; I had foreseen the section on contour containing Ottoman works on paper. And no doubt there were examples from other cultures which would have made a stronger case for *The Primacy of Drawing*.

During my researches, I have looked at the past with the unashamed bias of the present practitioner and found that other artists had been there too; borrowing, restructuring, reinventing. What is clear to me after much looking and reading is that drawing is a more *deterministic* medium than the other vehicles of visual art. The directness and apparent simplicity of its means make for an accessibility and ease of appropriation which I would like to celebrate. Accordingly I have devised a loose typology of line to organise diverse works, and hope that the juxtapositions of works within these categories will be illuminating.

Apart from surprising similarities across space and time, what has particularly struck me has been the diversity of techniques and ways of drawing used by individual artists, historically and in the present. A contemporary artist such as Jasper Johns (unfortunately not represented here) has drawn, in his long career, with pen, pencil, graphite, charcoal, crayon, pastel, washed with ink, watercolour, lighter-fluid, gouache, graphite on a variety of supports, including plastic, and mixed his media with fluency and invention. The range used by artists from the past is equally great, within the parameters of what media were available at the time. Dürer, for example, used pen and different coloured inks, brush and ink or watercolour, silverpoint, metal point, charcoal, and heightened

4 REMBRANDT (1606-1669) *Landscape with a Man Sitting on a Sluice Gate*
The Board of Trustees of the Victoria & Albert Museum

drawings with body white or colour, working on plain and coloured papers, grounded papers and vellum. Even in the Renaissance, with its canons of technique appropriate to sequences of drawing within workshop practice, there is no squeamishness at mixing media and departing from orthodoxy. My assumptions about the contemporaneity of certain techniques and ways of drawing have been challenged; so, for example, I have included here a curious and intense Giovanni Battista Tiepolo *Oil Sketch of a Head* (ill.5) which shows a freedom of attack that seems amazingly modern and is very different in kind from his more familiar pen and wash sketches. Where it has been possible to exhibit more than one work of an artist, I have attempted to choose works of different techniques in order to illustrate range and variety of approach.

In this exhibition I have selected mainly graphic and monochromatic works. Where there are coloured drawings, such as the Holbein *Portrait of a Lady, Thought to be Anne Boleyn* (ill.23) the colour is subordinate to the contour. I have deliberately not chosen watercolours, or even trois-crayon drawings. The intention has been to concentrate on qualities of line and mark. But of course, I am fully aware of the problem: what is a drawing, and what is not; where does drawing begin and end?

Drawing is, by its very nature, fluid and concerned with movement in all its aspects. Primarily it is the movement of the hand and its extension of pen, quill, brush, chalk or lead which reveals the process of describing lines and its ideation. The difficulties of erasure implicit in most of its methods mean that lines are left in place as a record of the processes of the moving hand. Drawings are frequently part of a serial process – moving towards another state which might or might not end in a 'finished' painting, sculpture, building or artefact. This seriality extends to the historical continuum in a more categorical way than other art media because the connecting link between art of the past and the present has always been by the act of drawing; less so, in the twentieth century. (Picasso's drawn *oeuvre* however, reads like an eclectic commentary on history reformulated for the 20th century.) Mobility is also inherent in the 'drawing out' of ideas from the mind in the conceptual, generative sketch; or the 'drawing from' nature or the model in the perceptual, observational drawing.

The teleology of drawing

11

Most exhibitions or commentaries on modern drawings do not attempt any limitation on the interpretation of drawing, and show free sketches in any medium, or collage, or even worked photographs or transferred images. An exhibition entitled *The Drawings of Anish Kapoor* at the Tate during 1990 showed unmediated stains and textures of paint on paper, reminiscent perhaps of Leonardo's 'clouds and patchy walls' before they gave 'rise to beautiful inventions of varied things.' In an age where painting aspires to the condition of drawing, that is, where spontaneity, fragmentation and immediacy are privileged, the designation *drawing* seems only a matter of degree: it is perhaps more irresolute or intimate than a painting, or simply executed on paper and not canvas.

Yet the sketches of the past, the *primi pensieri* or 'first thoughts' of artists, contain these very attributes of immediacy, intimacy, revelation and fragmentation. Vasari described them: 'Sketches ... are made in the form of a blotch, and are put down by us only as a rough draft of the whole. Out of the artist's impetuous mood they are hastily thrown off, with pen or other drawing instrument or with charcoal, only to test the spirit of that which occurs to him ...'[1] Reynolds reflected a historic valuation of such drawings when he wrote in Discourse XI: 'Those who are not conversant in works of art, are often surprised at the high value set by connoisseurs on drawings which appear careless, and in every respect unfinished.' And in Discourse VIII: 'From a slight undetermined drawing, where the ideas of the composition and character are, as I may say, only just touched upon, the imagination supplies more than the painter himself, probably, could produce; and we accordingly often find that the finished work disappoints the expectation that was raised from the sketch ...'[2]

Investigation of drawing has been divided between 'connoisseurship' (a very weazle word these days) and art history. The difference of approach as much as anything has to do with the emphasis of connoisseurs or collectors on appreciating a drawing in its own right (as long as its provenance holds water), and the insistence by art historians that drawings are serially linked within a causal chain. Most scholarly exegeses on drawings – and the New Art History has not as yet concerned itself much with drawing, perhaps because of its political rejection of notions of authorship and of isolating medium from idea – are devoted to questions of attribution, affiliation, chronology and hierarchy. It is always with

[1] Book XVI of *Vasari on Technique*, trans. Louisa S. Maclehose, Dover Publications, New York, 1960, p. 212

[2] Sir Joshua Reynolds, *Discourses on Art*, Intro. by Robert R. Wark, Collier Books, New York, 1966, pp. 175 and 145

regret that art historians announce that they cannot link a particular drawing with a work in another medium (the hierarchical value of painting or sculpture over drawing is implicit in this scenario), and must settle for a drawing being autonomous.

In the West, the uses of drawings have changed more over time than the means. By uses I mean the part drawing plays in the production of art, for example the Renaissance classification of first sketch, figure and drapery studies, compositional studies, *modello* or presentation drawing, cartoon and *sinopia* (the outline drawing which precedes a fresco) etc. which defined different stages in workshop production. (The uses of drawing for print media and sculpture have a different history.) There have been periods where preparatory compositional drawings or presentation drawings became unpopular, or artists have responded to market demand for particular types of drawing – Tiepolo's sketches, Millet's peasant studies, Wyndham Lewis' portrait drawings.

The 'uses' of drawing are multifarious, and it would be pointless to try and list them, in relation to a particular practice, or the cultural ethos which has shaped and inflected that practice. But it does seem that the autonomous drawing, which is not part of a serial developmental process and does not fulfill an outside commission – though it might very well fulfill, or initiate an internal brief – has always been produced by artists. And artists have continually rediscovered traditional uses of drawings as well as inventing new ones; Eisenstein's drawings for film, for example.

Artists seem to return to drawing in transitional phases in their development, after a period out of the studio or in times of doubt and crisis, as a medium of rediscovery and reaffirmation. Drawing is used 'to get one's hand in', and art students are encouraged to draw or work on paper when they are 'stuck' in other media. Philip Guston's career, where a long period of crisis led through drawing to an invigoration of creativity, is well documented in this respect.[3] (It is possible that the narrative of this mythological 'rebirth' accounts for his overriding importance to post-modern artists in the 1980s). It would also seem, on a more general level, that periods of questioning and crisis in art have been accompanied by a revival and intensification of drawing. The period of flux after the first World War led to a great efflorescence of drawing and we are presently witnessing a similar revival.[4]

The uses of drawing

[3] Magdalena Dabrowski, *The Drawings of Philip Guston*, The Museum of Modern Art, New York, 1988
[4] The appointment of the first Professor of Drawing at the Royal College of Art has occasioned much discussion in the Press about the revival of drawing. In particular, an article by Andrew Graham-Dixon in The Independent, 22 January 1991 and follow-up correspondence.

13

6 SIR EDWARD LUTYENS
Triumphal Arch c. 1923
British Architectural Library
Drawings Collection, Royal
Institute of British Architects

5 I interpret the persistence of this narrative in the field of drawing, but not painting or sculpture, to the value students put on drawing as a private and revelatory act which must remain sacrosanct
6 Petra ten-Doesschate Chu, Chapter entitled 'The Evolution of Realist and Naturalist Drawing', in *The Realist Tradition: French Painting and Drawing 1830-1900*, ed. Gabriel P. Weisberg, Cleveland Museum of Art, Indiana University Press, Cleveland 1980 pp 21 and 36
7 Richard Thomson, 'Impressionism and Drawing in the 1880s' in *Impressionist Drawings from British Public and Private Collections*, Christopher Lloyd and Richard Thomson, Arts Council and Phaidon Press, Oxford 1986, p. 49
8 Bernice Rose, *Drawing Now*, The Museum of Modern Art, New York 1976, p.9

Contemporary artists continue to make 'finished' presentation drawings. Richard Serra, for example, works on an enormous scale in charcoal. These are in no way preparatory drawings for sculpture, but reaffirmations of sculptural forms enlivened by texture, directed to an outside audience. I have observed that sculptors whose work depends on elaborate processes of outside fabrication, rather than 'hands on' assemblage of materials, such as sculptor Michael Sandle, tend to make finished drawings of the idealised work, as well as the initial sketches or working drawings. Although there is no system to these sculptors' drawings, they reflect the serial processes used by architecture and product design from first sketch (ill.6) to plan, elevation, projection, working drawing and client presentation drawing, even when the later stages happen on a computer. It is significant in this context that architectural practices depend on groups of professionals collaborating under the aegis of a 'house style' or dominant principal, not totally unlike the art workshops of the past; there is surely a connection between systematization of drawing process and methodologies of production.

The notion of systematization in drawing as a restrictive practice is one of the grand myths of the twentieth century. For some curious reason, the bogey of the repressive academy is as fresh to post-modernist students in art schools in 1991 as it was to post-Impressionists in 1891.[5] Historians of drawing in the 19th century admit that in spite of the Beaux Arts stranglehold on drawing instruction (graded exercises from model books and drawing from plaster casts to drawing from life, and from outline drawing to light and shade; from observation to idealisation etc.), French Realist drawing was characterised by 'an extraordinary diversity in individual drawing styles' and uses.[6]

The above author ends her chapter with 20th century complacency: 'Realist draftsmen ... won for drawing the independence and freedom that twentieth-century artists would generally take for granted.' Impressionist drawing, too, it is claimed by another author '... ceased to be a peripheral activity limited to preparatory work or immediate observation.'[7] This is a common claim. Bernice Rose writes in her introduction to *Drawing Now*: 'Drawing has moved from one context, that of a "minor" support medium, an adjunct to painting and sculpture, to another, that of a major and independent medium with distinctive expressive possibilities altogether its own,'[8] though she also admits that 'drawing has relinquished none of its traditional functions.'

The idea that 20th century drawing is much freer, and somehow different in kind from other periods seems to fly in the face of the evidence. It could be argued that even specialist drawing historians extrapolate from the generally accepted notions of the history of painting and sculpture when making such assessments. *I would propose that drawing constitutes a super-text (definitely not a sub-text) to the history of art.* The external conventions of usage and style of drawing are held in a different nexal relation to intention[9] and personal expression from painting and sculpture.

In juxtaposing a drawing by Cézanne (described categorically by Bernice Rose as the author of modern drawing[10] (ill.42) with a study from the Studio of Tintoretto (ill.7) to illustrate my point, I'm aware of Baxandall's warning about the dangers of false friends, as well as the existence of art-historical links. Baxandall writes: 'Many pictures ... are enclosed in a terrible varnish or carapace of false familiarity which ... is difficult to break through. This may be partly a matter of the museum-without-walls syndrome, but it is even more a matter of the medium of the art, the fact that most of us are not ... skilled executants in the medium. The contrast with language, a medium in which we are all incredibly skilled executants, is the most obvious. We find old language immediately remote because of its difference from the medium we use ourselves.'[11] If, on the other hand, the skilled executants in the medium of drawing do not find strangeness or remoteness in the drawings of the past or other cultures but freely borrow and reinvent them, is one arguing for a universal ignorance on the part of artists or a universally accessible sign language of drawing?

Norman Bryson writes: 'the sign projects itself historically; it throws itself forward in space and time ... This gives to thinking and writing about signs a necessary mandate to *go on* interpreting works of art beyond the context of their making.'[12] Artists clearly do exercise the mandate of continually reinterpreting works of art for their own purposes. However, they make scant distinction between material from the everyday environment and mediated material from the cultural realm, in their voracious appetite for plundering sources of visual imagery.

7 STUDIO OF JACOPO TINTORETTO (1518-1594)
Studies of Antique Sculpture (verso)
The Governing Body,
Christ Church, Oxford

[9] I am using 'intention' here in the wide sense defined by Michael Baxandall in Chapter ll of *Patterns of Intention*, Yale University Press, 1985: 'Every brushstroke is intentional in the sense that it has been made by a man (sic) whose skills and dispositions have developed in the course of purposeful activity. The fact that a brushstroke may have been unreflectively made does not isolate it from [such] skills ...' p.67
[10] Bernice Rose, *A Century of Modern Drawing from The Museum of Modern Art New York*, British Museum Publications, 1982, p.10. 'It is in this context that Cézanne's late watercolours began the history of modern drawing.'
[11] Michael Baxandall, ibid, pp. 114-115
[12] Norman Bryson, 'Semiology and Visual Interpretation' in *Visual Theory: Painting & Interpretation*, ed. Norman Bryson, Polity Press, Oxford, 1990, p.72

The enormous range of drawing media used by present and past artists is often in contrast to the concentrated mode in which they paint. One could postulate a theory of compensation – that the greater the stylistic restrictions of painting, the more the artist has the need for experimentation and freedom in drawing. Van Dyck, Romney and Guercino were a revelation to me in this respect: the extraordinary range of George Romney's wonderfully free sketches, (ill.8), the passionate intensity of Anthony van Dyck's compositional ink drawings, the invention and flexibility of Guercino's pen and ink drawings (ill.27) present a marked contrast to their Grand Manner paintings. Significantly, Van Dyck's and Guercino's handling of chalk, particularly stumped (rubbed and softened) red chalk, is less autographic and revelatory than their pen and ink drawings, (or ink and wash, or ink over outline chalk.) The 'soft' medium of chalk in some way masks expressivity – partly because it is historically loaded, partly because of its technical determinacy. Charcoal has replaced chalk in the modern canon as the popular soft medium, though for different purposes: it very readily provides surface integration, a spurious intensity and generously masks ineptitude. And it looks the real thing!

8 GEORGE ROMNEY (1734-1802)
A Shepherd Boy Asleep,
Watched by his Dog
The Syndics of the Fitzwilliam
Museum, Cambridge

16

It is tempting to take this speculation further and propose that the closer a drawing approaches a finished painting – the more it sublimates its brief– the more it is subject to the hegemony of sanctioned style. I'm aware that what we term the personal or autographic is deeply inflected by the culture which produced it; just as encoded as our restrospective readings of it. Nevertheless, the extraordinary correspondences of Romney's brush drawing *Two Young Girls Talking* (ill.17) with the Matisse brush-line *Tête* (ill.18) and the total chasm between their paintings of any period points to the significance of the *genre* of drawing as a meeting place for artists outside of the specificity of period.

9 GUERCINO (1591-1666) *Hercules and the Hydra*, Trustees of the British Museum

I have referred already to the notion of the determinacy of technique in drawing. This is a very simple concept. Whereas paint is a transformative medium – the artist can make of it what he or she will – drawing is a far more prescriptive medium, and asserts its linearity and technique however it is used. This applies particularly to pen and ink, or to the soft or wet media when used linearly, i.e. with a sharp or flexible point. When chalks or pastels are 'stumped' and their *sfumato* or *morbidezza*[13] effects exploited, they approximate much more to painting, and enter the realm of the suggestive and the transformative.

The range of effects which can be expressed in paint cannot be achieved in one technique of drawing, however fluent the artist. Consequently the artist either draws serially, or uses mixed media as an approximation, or a spur to discovery. Artists often bemoan the fact that they cannot achieve in painting the effects they have admired in their drawings, or prefer to work on paper (Paula Rego, for example, mounts her paper on to canvas or board) to avoid the terror of canvas.

Each of the drawing techniques has just so many possibilities of usage and the artist therefore chooses to use one or another of them appropriate to the intention of the drawing. When Dürer wished to express the anguish of a crucified Christ, *Head of the Dead Christ* (cover illustration) he chose to use charcoal because of its expressive capabilities; when he did preparatory sketches for an engraving *Study of Eve* (ill.18), he chose pen and ink as the closest equivalent medium for describing the contours and controlled hatching of the body. Marcel Roethlisberger observes a similar specificity in Claude Lorrain's working methods: 'a small leaf from a sketchbook, a first *pensée* for a picture, a representative pictorial drawing or a page from the *Liber*, all command a proper medium and a different degree of elaboration. A view of undergrowth demands the soft work of pen and brush, an architectural study is best carried out in sharp penwork, a sheep in chalk.'[14]

Certain print means have evolved because of their closeness to drawing technique, as much as the need to extend the communicative uses of drawing. Aquatint, for example, was developed by Goya because of its potential for imitating the subtleties of wash drawing, and was used in copy-books of 'famous' drawings for the same reasons. It is interesting how print requirements feed back into preparatory drawings. Dürer's pen at times seems to imitate the action of the buren, in the way it is

10 ALBRECHT DÜRER (1471–1528)
Study of Eve
Trustees of the British Museum

18

flicked up at the end of a line, which is how the buren is controlled in order not to grave too deeply into the plate at the end of a long stroke; similarly he eschews elaborate cross-hatching which would fill up with ink in printing. Bernardo Parentino's curious and complex *Allegory, in Imitation of an Antique Relief* (ill. 11) is indistinguishable from an engraving; even the awkwardness of drawing suggests the kind of distortion which results from tracing over a previous drawing.

11 BERNARDO PARENTINO
(1437–1531)
An Allegory, in Imitation of an Antique Relief
The Governing Body,
Christ Church, Oxford

[13] These are related terms. *Sfumato* is the technique of softening outlines to form imperceptible transitions 'like smoke', and *morbidezza* is the term for the delicate fusion of tones in rendering soft flesh.
[14] Marcel Roethlisberger, *Claude Lorrain: The Drawings*, University of California Press, 1968, p.24

The drawing media might be limited, but they are certainly not inflexible. Determinacy occurs within an enormous spectrum of possibilities. The range of skills of a practising artist become so internalised that choice of medium only becomes conscious when new parameters of experimentation are entered into. The question of how an artist renders line personal, however, is a slightly different matter. Autograph has always been central to discussions and evaluation of drawing, beginning with Pliny's account of the visit of Apelles to Protogenes. [15]

'We must pick out what is good for us where we can find it – except from our own works. I have a horror of copying myself. But when I am shown a portfolio of old drawings, for instance, I have no qualms about taking anything I want from them.' Picasso [16]

It is interesting that Picasso talks about copying *drawings* in the above quote, because when one thinks about copying it is usually with the mental picture (a slightly faded, sepia image) of students with their easels in front of paintings in the Louvre. Yet artists have always copied drawings more than paintings (for evaluative reasons as much as ease of access) and the medium of copying, of transferring cultural property, is primarily that of drawing. Although the term 'copying' as reproduction, has pejorative implications nowadays, the practice of referring back to the past has been as constantly revived in the 20th century as in preceding periods. The importance attached to copying in history has seldom been naïve; the writings of artists reveal an understanding of it as a means towards internalising the past in order to mobilise present practice.

To a large extent traditional art history, obsessed with questions of authenticity, has privileged the revelation of autograph in the analysis of artists' drawings, giving importance to the question of copying within the context of development of personal (or workshop) style. While, of course, I do not deny the latter mechanism, I am proposing a more fundamental issue about the primacy of drawing. Painting or sculpture are relatively *closed* systems: as the distillation or synthesis of the preceding stages. Drawing, on the other hand, in its fragmentation and seriality – its forward impetus – is *open* to appropriation, both as act and subject.

It seems to me interesting that the practice of recording a painterly *oeuvre* is still used by some 20th century artists (Gwyther

[15] William Hogarth embellishes the story in the Preface to 'The Analysis of Beauty' 1753, p.xviii: 'Apelles having heard of the fame of Protogenes, went to Rhodes to pay him a visit, but not finding him at home asked for a board, on which he drew a Line, telling the servant maid, that line would signify to her master who had been to see him. .....Protogenes when he came home took the hint, and drew a finer or rather more expressive line within it, to shew Apelles if he came again, that he understood his meaning.'
[16] 'Conversations with Picasso' by Christian Zervos, trans. in *The Painter's Object*, ed. Myfanwy Evans, Gerald Howe Ltd, London, 1937, p.85

Irwin, for example), photography notwithstanding. Rubens did so, and Claude made a complete record of his *oeuvre* in the *Liber Veritatis*. Commentators make much of the discrepancy between his 'copies' and the finished work. This doesn't seem to me puzzling: drawing a finished work is an act of re-appropriation, opening up the sealed work to possibilities of re-use.

Artists apprenticed to workshops – in India or Japan as much as Europe – have been schooled to work like their masters or mistresses. The sport of art history has been to disentangle Leonardo from Verrocchio, or 'follower of Kuniyoshi' from Kuniyoshi. In drawings – where admittedly there is far less circumstantial evidence than in painting or sculpture – the difficulties of attribution are much greater. The problems of attribution around the drawings of Rembrandt – who was renowned as a teacher – and his students, are immense and ongoing. The disentangling of Van Dyck's and Rubens' drawings is another minefield; a recent publication, Alexander Perrig's *The Science of Attribution*[17] has reshuffled a number of previously uncontroversial Michelangelo drawings on to the sidelines. As many 20th century artists as historic have been subject to forgeries of their drawings. Why should this be so, if line is as autographic, as personally expressive as claimed?

Rubens' habit of working over other artists' drawings – the apotheosis of appropriation! – has proved an embarrassing narrative for historians, lacking as it apparently does the political message of Rauschenberg rubbing out a drawing by De Kooning in 1953, and implying scant respect for other artists. Yet there are numerous apocryphal tales of masters correcting their pupils' drawings, and prodigy pupils having their come-uppance by correcting the master's drawing. (There are shades of kingship mythology here; I haven't come across any references to women in similar scenarios). Rubens made sure of putting the 'finishing strokes' on his workshop productions as the authenticating marks of valorisation. Would Duchamp have drawn an autographic moustache on to the real Mona Lisa painting, one wonders?

I believe that what is missing from the accounts of authenticity is the possibility that autograph is not ensured in every line, but is intermittent. The encyclopaedic nature of drawing within an artist's *oeuvre* means that in some drawings autograph has been suppressed, overlaid or not yet formulated. To insist on the Apelles/Protogenes narrative – that every drawing must carry the stamp of its author – is either naïve or pandering to an economist view of art.

12 PETER PAUL RUBENS (1577-1640) *Abel Slain by Cain* The Syndics of the Fitzwilliam Museum, Cambridge

13 SIR ANTHONY VAN DYCK (1599-1641) *Study for the Lamentation* Trustees of the British Museum

[17] Alexander Perrig, *Michelangelo's Drawings: The Science of Attribution*, Yale University Press, New Haven and London, 1991

21

[18] Jean-Baptiste Simeon Chardin, 'Art is Long', quoted in Robert Goldwater and Marco Treves, eds, *Artists on Art*, John Murray, London, 1976, p.169

[19] Sir Joshua Reynold, Discourse XV, ibid, p.238

[20] The re-introduction of figure drawing into British art school curricula because of student insistence was just such an act of reversal. The problem remains that the majority of tutors, institutionalised in the 1960s cannot instruct students how to apply life drawing to their general practice.

[21] Quoted in Julius S. Held, *Rubens: Selected Drawings*, Phaidon, Oxford, 1986, p.16

The value of drawing

The *academie*, the presentation drawing of the Beaux Arts or Academy school represents the triumph of style over autograph; of idealised product over gesture. The procedures towards this end (socialising the brute artist) were an admixture of acquisition of institutionalised skills accompanied by stages of autographic loss. How aspiring students like Chardin 'withered for days and nights before immobile and inanimate nature'[18], unless they had Reynolds' kind dispensation for comfort: 'perhaps every Student must not be strictly bound to general methods, if they strongly thwart the peculiar turn of his own mind.'[19] In contemporary art schools in Britain the process whereby students are encouraged to lose the 'academic' pencil drawing skills they have acquired at school and discover personal expression is not so much a reversal of the former system, as the shadow side of authoritarian practice. It is equally manipulative. But the will to draw is so insistent, that in both scenarios the freedom of the artist to seek other affiliations and to experiment doesn't seem impaired in the long run.[20]

'... the drawings which he had collected and made he ordered to be held and preserved for the benefit of any of his sons who would want to follow him in the art of painting, or, failing such, for the benefit of any of his daughters who might marry a recognised painter.' (sic!) Rubens' Will[21]

Artists' evaluation of drawing in the West has not changed much over the centuries. We know that the drawings of art-workshops were collected as a valuable resource, and as such willed to heirs, catalogued and acquired by other artists. In later periods collections of drawings were bequeathed to the state by artists or their heirs, to academic institutions and museums, who reciprocally recognised the significance of drawing as a study resource for artists. Artists were among the first commoners admitted to the art collections of princes in France (they were usually expected to produce copies) and they were given special privileges in the Louvre when it was founded. Academies and art schools have been associated with drawings collections, such as the South Kensington Museum design and drawing resource for the South Kensington School of Art (now respectively the Victoria & Albert Museum and The Royal College of Art).

As well as copying other artists' drawings, exchanging drawings with other artists (Raphael and Dürer, for example) artists have assembled collections, sometimes commissioning professional pattern-book copyists and engravers to make up portfolios for studio use. Artists' collections of drawings, culminating in the great 18th century British collections of Lawrence, Lely and Reynolds, have been the spur to connoisseurship. The great private drawings collections of Europe (some of which passed to the state), largely came from atelier collections, or works bought from artists' studios through the mediation of dealers. Even in the United States, the history of Old Master drawing stems from a collection imported by a portrait painter, John Smibert.

Artists have endlessly theorised about the meaning of drawing, as well as writing practical manuals. Cennini, Vasari, Piero della Francesca, Dürer, Federigo Zuccaro, Reynolds, Hogarth, Ruskin, Paul Klee – the list is endless.

The value of drawing as a continuous exercise has always been part of the artistic *gestalt* – from Cennini's exhortations 'Do not fail ... to draw something every day, for no matter how little it is it will be well worth while, and will do you a world of good'[22] to present art practice formulated in art schools. Likewise the practice of filling (and valuing) sketchbooks has been continuous from Pisanello to Picasso and beyond.

The importance of drawing to artists is not only a feature of the West. In India where princes and patrons did not particularly value study drawings or sketches, the survival of these works has been ensured by their significance for the atelier.

[22] Cennino d'Andrea Cennini, Chapter XXVIII, *Il Libro dell' Arte* trans. Daniel V. Thompson, Jr, Dover Publications, New York, 1960, p.15

14 RAJASTHAN, SAWAR SCHOOL
Page of Sketches c. 1700
Collection Howard Hodgkin,
London

'Such material ... remained in the workshops of the artists, who passed it on to their descendants in the same way that other Indian craftsmen transmitted tools and trade secrets to their sons and grandsons'[23] Nevertheless, finished drawings, particularly portraits, were commissioned in great numbers and assembled in princely albums. The uses of drawing in courtly India are not that different from the West: there exist pages of sketchbooks with trial ideas for compositions (both secular and religious) and observational sketches which exactly parallel Western practice (ill.14); autonomous line and wash drawings, presumably produced for the artist's own use or enjoyment; under-drawings for finished works; cartoons for wall paintings; pounced drawings for transfer and copy drawings. (In the latter context it is worth noting that in the 17th century, there are Moghul copies of Western art in India contemporaneous with Rembrandt's copies of Moghul miniatures in Holland.)

In China and Japan where the great traditions of painting embodied graphic skills, practice drawings were not valued by patrons. It is Western collectors who have demarcated the area of Japanese 'drawing' (as opposed to brush painting), which is still not particularly esteemed in Japan. The 17th, 18th and 19th century preliminary sketches circulating in the West are mainly from the collections of pupils and heirs of artistic workshops (ill.15).

I have pursued this list at some length in order to bring home the point that no matter how academics have carved up the history of art into styles, periods, influences and isms, the primal activity of drawing is a constant in artistic production, and esteemed by artists outside of market valorisation. This estimation might have a negative formulation, such as Michelangelo destroying drawings so they wouldn't fall into other hands because they were too revealing.

Marcel Roethlisberger claims that Claude 'valued his drawings lightly'[24] because he gave them away as gifts; one would assume, on the contrary, that to give something rather than sell it implies a different order of value. Claude's estate contained 1100 drawings; hardly a 'light'ness of elbow-room.

A critic at my house sees some paintings. Greatly perturbed, he asks for my drawings. My drawings? Never! They are my letters, my secrets.

Paul Gauguin[25]

[23] Stuart Cary Welch, *Indian Drawings and Painted Sketches: 16th through 19th Centuries* The Asia Society in association with John Weatherhill, New York, 1976, p. 14
[24] Marcel Roethlisberger, ibid p. 8
[25] Paul Gauguin, from the 'Intimate Journals', quoted in Robert Goldwater and Marco Treves, eds. *Artists on Art*, John Murray, London 1976, p. 374

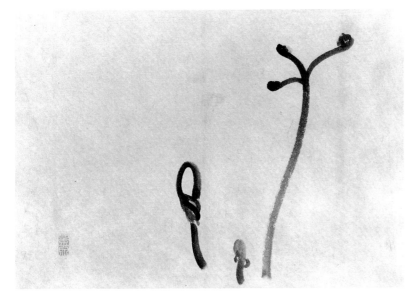

15 MATSUMURA KEIBUN
Bracken c. 1820
Collection of Mr and Mrs Dennis Wiseman

The organisation of the drawings in this exhibition into categories has arisen out of my ideas about determinacy of line and its appropriateness to certain kinds of drawing. Categorisation is a very imprecise exercise – perhaps a futile one, except in so far as it gives shape to a body of material – because some drawings could equally happily fit into three or four different contexts, others totally defy any attempt to push them around! I have attempted to isolate the most significant confluence of technique, subject and use to place works, but attempts to read intention are inevitably very personal. I have also tried to take on board the question of omission: what is left out of a drawing is a question of skill and choice, and just as significant as what is drawn.

I have not grouped works by technique or iconography, nor have I respected period or culture. There is no intention of negating distinctions between drawings of different times and traditions; but there is an attempt to find correspondences between works from different contexts in support of notions of the primacy of drawing.

DEANNA PETHERBRIDGE

A brush can produce the finest of hair lines in the hands of a skilled Western miniaturist or a Moghul artist, with variations of thickness almost invisible to the naked eye. Generally we admire brush drawings for their flexibility of stroke and the ease of sweeping line.

A brush stroke with ink makes a very different mark when it is loaded or dry, or the hairs are allowed to separate and leave slight tracings in response to changes of pressure, as in the Matisse *Visage* of 1951 (ill.18) This is a schematic outline drawing, and the calligraphic qualities of brush are exploited playfully in the curves of the hair and the parted lips. Romney's drawing *A Shepherd Boy Asleep Watched by his Dog at the Approach of a Thunderstorm* (ill.8) depends on an interplay between brush strokes made with the point of the brush, fuller strokes using the whole weight of the brush and the dragged effects of a dry brush. The hesitant black chalk under-drawing is overwhelmed by the fluency of the brush-work, as in his drawing *Two Young Girls Talking* (ill.17) which is very close in spirit to the Matisse. Nicholaes Maes' *A Milkseller at a House Door,* within the Rembrandt tradition, depends on the broken surface and vitality of a dragged brush dipped in brown ink, in a keenly observed *genre* scene (ill.20).

The Zen brush drawing by Isshi of *A Contemplative Figure* (ill.19) explores within a very small drawing the range and subtlety of monochrome brush technique; not very far from Claude Lorrain's *A Woodland Glade* (ill.16), one of his free and lyrical sketches from nature. Historically in the West, monochrome brush and ink technique, because it pertains to 'drawing' rather than 'painting' seems to allow a far greater freedom than the related technique of watercolour. Claude celebrates the luminosity and transparency of ink and the tonal range of wash. The surface deposit which can give a slightly metallic quality to ink wash (if the paper is not too absorbant) imparts a richness which watercolour can never achieve without losing its transparency.

The flexible brush

16 CLAUDE LORRAIN (1600–82) *Woodland Glade*
Sepia wash over black chalk, 20.5 x 27.2cm, Trustees of the British Museum

17 GEORGE ROMNEY (1734-1802) *Two Young Girls Talking*
Brush with dark brown watercolour wash over pencil, 34.3 x 21cm
The Syndics of the Fitzwilliam Museum, Cambridge

18 HENRI MATISSE *Visage* 1951
Brush and indian ink, 43.5 x 33.5cm, Libby Howie and John Pillar Fine Art
© Succession H. Matisse/DACS 1991

19 ISSHI BUNSHU *Zen Drawing of a Contemplative Figure* c. 1640
Brush and ink, 27.1 x 18.6cm, Collection of Mr and Mrs Dennis Wiseman

20 NICHOLAS MAES (1634-1693) *A Milkseller at a House Door*
Pen and wash, 15.2 x 18.7cm, The Syndics of the Fitzwilliam Museum, Cambridge

Outline drawing, where detail is supressed or subjugated to the containing and defining contour, is the most conceptual means of drawing. It is also the most abstract, in the sense that to arrive at a clarity of outline is a process of reduction and deliberate simplification and stylisation. Artists such as Ingres produced many preliminary sketches before arriving at the final contour drawing.

In addition to this process of technical attrition, drawings of pure contour are reductive in other ways; all extraneous detail is stripped away, and usually there is a rigorous approach to the iconography, in order to fix on the most telling and simplified imagery. The space contained within an outline is often empty of incident, but if we are familiar with its conventions, we read body or object, or abstract form. Being the most schematic, the reductive outline drawing is therefore the most encoded.

Philip Rawson writes in *Drawing* about works which accept the basic integrity of silhouette: 'It may seem that such art actually preaches discipline as a virtue, and it is associated with the social ideal of discipline.'[1] The Jaipuri drawing *Portrait of Pratap Singh of Jaipur as Prince and Ruler* (ill.22), is just such a disciplined drawing, and like the Hans Holbein the Younger *Portrait of a Lady, Thought to be Anne Boleyn* (ill.23) allows for an emphatic line here and there as a counterpoint to the very fine outlines. Both portrait drawings depend on the most subtle interventions within the face and head-dress, but the containment of outline remains paramount.

Percy Wyndham Lewis in the *Portrait of Miss E* (ill.21) also concentrates detail in the head, but the portrait description is continued in the use of rocking curves in the stylish half-reclining figure.

[1] Philip Rawson, *Drawing* Oxford University Press, London 1969, p.97

The classic contour

21 PERCY WYNDHAM LEWIS *Portrait of Miss E* 1920
Pencil, 38 x 56cm, Manchester City Art Galleries

22 JAIPURI SCHOOL *Portrait of Pratap Singh of Jaipur as Prince and Ruler*
Chalk and ink with pointed brush, touched with white, 57.5 x 71cm
Collection Howard Hodgkin, London

23 HANS HOLBEIN THE YOUNGER (1497/8-1543) *Portrait of a Lady, Thought to be Anne Boleyn*
Black chalk, partly stumped, and red chalk;
brush and black ink, yellow wash on pink prepared paper, 23.6 x 29.8cm
Trustees of the British Museum

The fulsome serpentine or baroque line has been particularly admired in certain periods of Western art history and has formed part of an ongoing debate polarised around Michelangelo, Rubens and Corregio in opposition to Raphael and Dürer. Hogarth exalted the superior values of the 'serpentine' line in his *Analysis of Beauty* of 1753, and the red chalk drawing by Guercino, *Hercules Slaying the Hydra* (ill.9) has a monster, very close to the serpent Laocoon from which Hogarth took his terminology.

Cursive drawings tend to be in pen or quill and ink, pencil or sharpened chalk, the instruments of calligraphy, and sometimes wash is used to give depth or accent to the drawing. The sketchbook leaf attributed to Agostino Carracci, *Studies with the Head of an Eagle and Men's Profiles and Caricatures* (ill.24) shows exercises in free pen and ink cursive drawing which is very close to writing; a flamboyant calligraphy enjoyed four centuries later by Emilio Greco in his *Head of a Girl* (ill.26). Dürer (capable of a range of drawing equalled only by Picasso) contrasts the calligraphic proliferation of contours of musculature in legs and arms in his *Study of Eve* (ill.10) with the silhouetted outline of the figure against a flat wash background. This is one of a group of preparatory drawings for an engraving of Adam and Eve, and although the pen is calligraphic in the contour rhythms, the intent of the final medium has conditioned the use of hatching.

The sinuous line can be the line of discovery, with shapes scribed and reinscribed in search of telling form, as in the black chalk cartoon by Elisabetta Sirani, *Head of the Virgin with a Halo of Stars* (ill.25). Some of the *pentimenti* or reconsidered lines have been obliterated with white chalk, others have been left to encircle the head, activating the halo of stars.

The sinuous line

24 AGOSTINO CARRACCI (1557–1602)
Sheet of Studies with the Head of an Eagle and Men's Profiles and Caricatures
Pen and brown ink and some wash, 14.6 x 20cm
Viscount Coke and the Trustees of the Holkham Estate

25 ELISABETTA SIRANI (1638–1665) *Head of the Virgin with a Halo of Stars*
Black chalk (with corrections in white chalk) on joined paper (cartoon), 47.2 x 36.8cm
The Governing Body, Christ Church, Oxford

26 EMILIO GRECO *Head of a Girl* 1954
Pen and ink, 49.8 x 35.6cm, Tate Gallery

The tradition of depicting landscape in drawing by clusters of repeated contours and shorthand squiggles of slow and quick linear rhythms, has a long history in southern and northern Europe. Guercino continues the usage of Fra Bartolomeo in his breezy *Landscape with Two Fishermen* (ill.25) where the bank and the trees with birds flying above them are indicated by cursory, but telling rhythmic lines full of *brio*. Edward Wadsworth's *Granite Quarries* (ill.29) is a very 20th century drawing, nevertheless it still uses a related rhythmic convention. The concentrated clusters of hatched line break up the surface of the drawing into the planes, declivities and sober patterns of the quarries.

Rhythmic drawing is not only related to landscape. It was the hallmark of the great 18th century Venetian draughtsmen, and activates Watteau's tiny red chalk drawing, *Back of a Female Figure* (ill.28). Here there is a wonderful marriage of rhythmic abstraction with the skills of representing texture and surface.

Line generating rhythm

27 GUERCINO (1591-1666) *Landscape with Two Fisherman*
Pen and brown ink, 15.8 x 19cm, Trustees of the British Museum

28 JEAN-ANTOINE WATTEAU (1684-1721) *Back of a Female Figure*
Red chalk, 13.7 x 7.9cm, The Syndics of the Fitzwilliam Museum, Cambridge

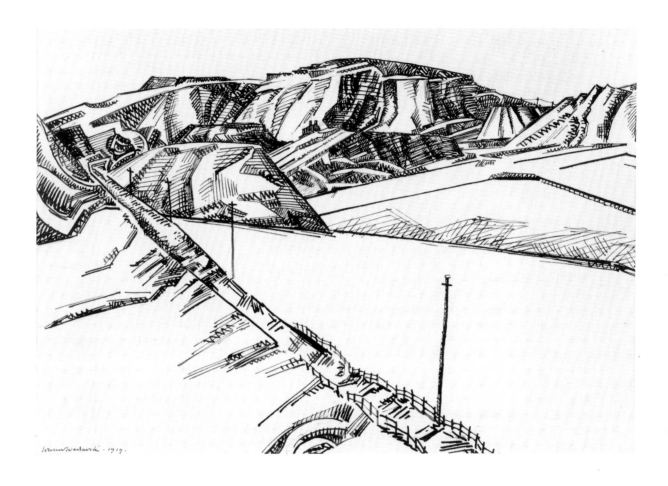

29 EDWARD WADSWORTH *Granite Quarries* 1919
Pen and ink, 25.3 x 36.7cm, Whitworth Art Gallery, University of Manchester

This is a rather rhetorical title, in order to convey the notion that the combination of pen and wash is a marriage of opposites: the hard with the soft, the linear with the painterly, the contained with the indeterminate. The pen or quill point graves into the paper fibres, whereas the wash floats and saturates. When the narrow deposit of the pen line is touched with water or wash, it spreads and bleeds; the brush marries it to the paper with a lyricism which pen cannot achieve as unadorned line, except by metaphoric strategies of repetitious rhythms or congruent contours.

Although the participation of paper within and around the linear formulation is an essential part of all drawings, it plays a slightly different role in an ink and wash drawing. Because of the subtlety of tonal gradation of ink-wash, the parts of the paper left untreated can read as highlight on a curved form, or daylight, as in Giovanni Battista Tiepolo's *Drawing of Farm Buildings* (ill.30), bathed in Mediterranean sun and heat. Moonlight is captured in Federigo Zuccaro's *A Man Drawing by Moonlight from the Window of a House,* (ill.31). This drawing is from a series depicting the life of Zuccaro's brother Taddeo. According to legend, the impecunious artist was forced to do menial tasks during the day and paint at night, but this sad story must be put in the context of a vogue for moonlight pictures. Some inks lighten with age, so presumably the brown shadowy interior was once more intense in relation to the splashes of moonlight on the artist's head and shoulders, and the shimmer of light on the river he is drawing through the open shutters. Silvery moonlight tactically lightens the head with its curious little cap, while the artist's backview melts into the shadowy room, with the legs revealed by the only lines used in the drawing.

The use of wash to pick out forms or strengthen shadows, or for purposes of differentiating texture and material is apparent in the complex architectural drawing *A Hall of State* (ill.32) from the School of the Galli-Bibiena, who specialised in stage sets and architectural studies.

30 GIOVANNI BATTISTA TIEPOLO (1696–1770) *Drawing of Farm Buildings*
Pen and bistre, 17 x 28.2cm, Trustees of the British Museum

31 FEDERICO ZUCCARO (1542-1609)
A Man Drawing by Moonlight from the Window of a House
Pen, brown ink and brown wash, 35.6 x 17.8cm
The Visitors of the Ashmolean Museum

32 SCHOOL OF GALLI-BIBIENA (18th century) *A Hall of State*
Pen and brown ink, grey and pink wash, 42.8 x 58cm, British Architectural Library Drawings Collection,
Royal Institute of British Architects

Until the advent of the lead pencil, pen and ink (or quill or reed pen) was the preferred medium for exploratory sketches in the West. The pen can produce a wide repertoire of dashes, strokes, blots, modulations of fine and thickened lines, delicacy of touch or weight of attack. Like the pencil, it traces the processes of exploration of an idea, records speed or hesitancy and readily reveals the mood and intensity of the artist. Some traditional inks (such as iron-gall ink) are very acid and spread and eat into the paper over time, so that the apparent drama of line in old drawings can be rather delusive.

Expressiveness of line is also generated in response to the subject matter, such as the slashed pencil rhythms of Sickert's *He Killed his Father in a Fight* (ill.34). Although the emotive quality of the blunt lead strokes is undeniable, the schema of this drawing is close to Rembrandt's *Jael and Sisera* study in the Ashmolean, which consciously or unconsciously has provided a model both for composition and treatment of a study of passion. The subject of the Christian Passion has engendered the anguish of Dürer's charcoal drawing *Head of the Dead Christ* (cover illustration). This is not a dashed-off sketch: the variation of treatment for the dramatically high-lighted face and the gothic rhythms of the beard reveal this drawing as a distillation of skills. The incorporation of the very large monogram and date into the composition forefronts the identification of the artist with the subject matter.

James Gillray's *Portrait of George Humphrey Jnr* (ill.33) was produced during a period of mental disturbance, which partly accounts for the fragmentation of line, although he appears not to have lost his mordant skills of caricature. The psychotic attack of Gillray's drawing is close to the scored lines of Leon Kossoff's contemporary drawing for *Woman Ill in Bed Surrounded by Family* (ill.35).

The expressive gesture

33 JAMES GILLRAY (1757–1815) *Portrait of George Humphrey Jnr*
Pen and ink, 37 x 49.2cm, Trustees of the British Museum

34 WALTER SICKERT (1860–1942) *He Killed his Father in a Fight*
Pencil, 23.6 x 29.8cm, Whitworth Art Gallery, University of Manchester

35 LEON KOSSOFF *Drawing for 'Woman Ill in Bed Surrounded by Family'* 1965
Pen and ink, 29.8 x 22.2cm, Tate Gallery

By a 'dumb' line, I mean a line which is not eloquent in the language of drawing. The artist ignores, or deliberately abnegates, niceties of drawing style in favour of roughness, 'childlike' simplicity, spontaneity or neutrality.

It is a line which, in the 20th century, owes much to Gauguin and his elevation of the bold 'primitive' contour which does not separate itself from colour. Paula Modersohn-Becker's *Sketch of a Peasant Girl* (ill.36) comes out of the Symbolist celebration of the primitive, and employs what she termed 'the naive in line' in her deceptively simple drawing.

Deliberately dumb line sometimes masks the skill of the artist; it also blurs distinctions between boundaries of media – the typical marks of pencil, charcoal and brush – in order to arrive at the essential line *qua* line. Sandro Chia appears deliberately to suppress autograph and style and medium specificity in the coloured drawing of a *Seated Male Figure* (ill.38)

Use of the dumb line does not negate expressive content; on the contrary it is a type of line which is occasionally chosen by executants of the highest skill as a form of mock-crudity in seeking a certain effect. In the black chalk drawing *Locos* (ill.37) by Francisco Goya, a master draughtsman of inexhaustible range, the roughness of the line has been chosen to underpin the crude sexuality of the subject.

The dumb line

36 PAULA MODERSOHN-BECKER (1867-1907) *Sketch of a Peasant Girl*
Charcoal, 18.7 x 22.5cm, The Board of Trustees of the Victoria & Albert Museum

37 FRANCISCO JOSE GOYA (1746–1828) *Locos*
Chalk, 19.1 x 14.4cm, Trustees of the British Museum

38 SANDRO CHIA (b. 1946) *Seated Male Figure*
Tempera and watercolour, 25.4 x 20.3cm, The Syndics of the Fitzwilliam Museum, Cambridge
© Sandro Chia/DACS, London, VAGA, New York, 1991

The point of analysis

There is a genus of drawing where the urge to analyse form or investigate the problematics of representation is at the forefront. Quality of line can be locked into this process of investigation, as in Paul Cézanne's fine and sensitive *Study from the Statuette of a Cupid* (ill.42), or become secondary to other priorities as in Tintoretto's *Christ on the Cross* (ill.43).

Geometry permeates the discourse of systematic analysis, and the geometric system of orthogonal projection, investigated by Piero della Francesca and Dürer, has been revived centuries later by Victor Newsome in *Profile Head* (ill.39).

Geometry is also the source of the constituent arcs and directional lines with which Cézanne analyses the planar volume and spatial recession of the little statuette of Cupid. Cézanne did many drawings from sculpture, as did Tintoretto, who had small wax models of Michelangelo's sculpture and casts from the antique in his studio. Cézanne's analysis of form is of the order of investigation which led to the Cubist movement: nevertheless it is very close to the rhythms in the *Two Studies of Antique Sculpture* from the Studio of Tintoretto (ill.7). Both drawings depend on sequences of overlapping arcs which never unite to form a discrete contour, but allow for passages of the paper to register as diffusing light (or unifying tonality in the Tintoretto studio drawing, which is on blue paper).

The Cubist stylisation of figures has inflected David Bomberg's drawing *Sappers at Work* (ill.40), not far away from the geometricized mannequins of Luca Cambiaso's *The Crucifixion* (ill.41). The use of a a diagonally defined pictorial space gives drama to both works, emphasized by the dramatic lights and darks in the case of the Bomberg drawing.

It is a common misconception that analytical procedures are antipathetic to feeling. The powerful *Christ on the Cross* by Jacopo Tintoretto is no less an emotive work for its schematic drawing (it has been squared up for transfer), and Victor Newsome achieves dramatic intensity in his drawing of a head in profile, allowing the distortions which arise out of the drawing method to acquire a strangeness and poignancy.

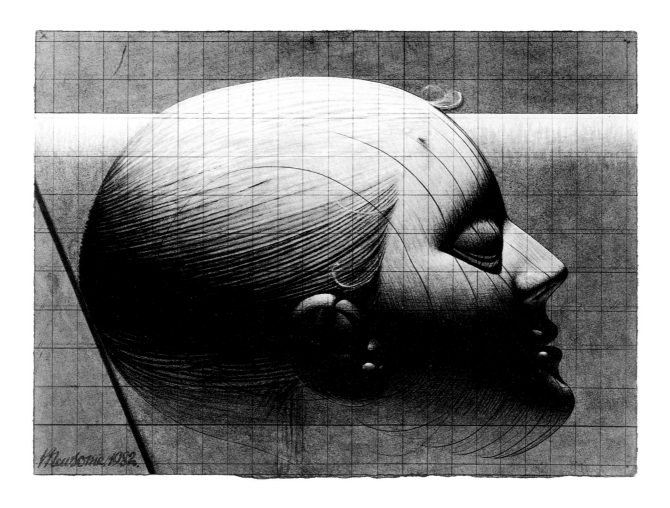

39 VICTOR NEWSOME *Profile Head* 1982
Pencil; grey wash, heightened with acrylic white, squared in pencil, 32.8 x 46cm
Trustees of the British Museum

40 DAVID BOMBERG *Sappers at Work* 1919
Charcoal, 67.5 x 56cm, The Trustees of the Imperial War Museum

41 LUCA CAMBIASO *The Crucifixion,* after 1570
Pen, brown ink and wash, 21.4 x 29.5cm, Whitworth Art Gallery, University of Manchester

42 PAUL CEZANNE *Study from the Statuette of a Cupid* c. 1890
Black chalk, 50.5 x 32.1cm, Trustees of the British Museum

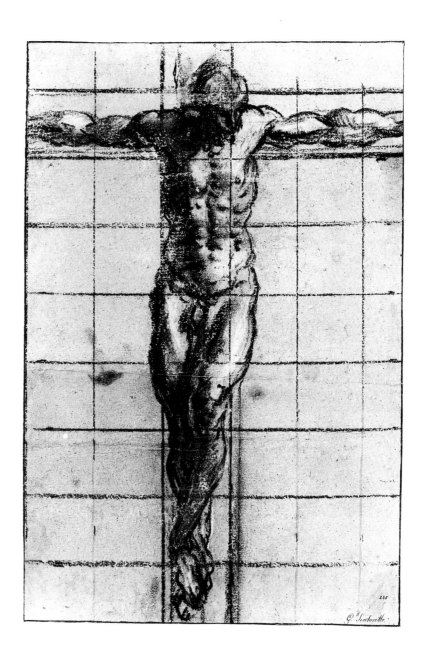

43 JACOPO TINTORETTO (1518-1594) *Christ on the Cross*
Black chalk heightened with white on grey paper, squared in black chalk, 23.6 x 29.8cm
The Board of Trustees of the Victoria & Albert Museum

Style is more important than autograph or expression in finished or presentation drawings, or those directed towards an external brief, such as portraiture. Traditionally the 'soft' media have been selected by artists when they wish to make a *modello* for a finished large-scale painting, a drapery study, a presentation drawing of a sculpture or architectural composition or a portrait likeness. The 'soft' media more readily convey light and shade, corporeality or tonal modulation. The use of coloured papers as a support to chalk or high-lighted drawings sets up a tonal scale which draws the work closer to painting, as in the deeply moving, and not overly finished, Van Dyck *Lamentation* (ill.21) on blue gray paper.

Head and Hands of a Weeping Mother from the Studio of Giulio Romano (ill.47) is a cartoon for a tapestry, intended to be reversed in the final work. Although the slightly crude contours and harshness of drawing accommodate the transformation of style and loss of autograph which imagery suffers when translated into another medium, it is a very powerful and arresting fragment.

The soft *sfumato* effects of chalk are handled with great mastery in the lyrical *Head of a Young Man* (ill.44) by Franciabigio, with touches of white highlighting the forward planes of forehead, nose and cheekbones. Similar effects are used by Bartolommeo Montagna in the beautiful stumped chalk or charcoal *Bust of the Virgin* (ill.48). The drawing is very rubbed, but the contrast between the softness of the facial modelling and the insistent curves and simplified forms of neckline and drapery are clear. Likewise in the *Portrait of Winifred John* (ill.46) by Gwen John, the head is treated in a different manner from the hair, scarf and torso. The specifics of portrait likeness here have called for a delicacy of touch and fineness of line in negotiating the rather idealised features, contrasted with the bold pencil rhythms of the blouse and scarf. The contrast is so marked that it suggests an ambivalence on the part of the artist either towards the sitter or the problematics of portraiture.

A silverpoint line, heightened with white, is used on the very fine *Head of a Boy in a Cap* by Lorenzo di Credi, where the modelling of the face is entirely linear.

Drawing to an end

44 FRANCIABIGIO *Head of a Young Man,* early 16th century
Black chalk with touches of white, 25.1 x 20.6cm, The Board of Trustees of the Victoria & Albert Museum

45 GWEN JOHN *Portrait of Winifred John* 1939
Pencil on buff paper, 15.9 x 15.9cm, Sheffield City Art Galleries

46 LORENZO DI CREDI (*c.* 1458–1537) *Head of a Boy in a Cap*
Silverpoint, heightened with white on buff-coloured ground, 23.6 x 29.8cm
The Governing Body, Christ Church, Oxford

47 STUDIO OF GIULIO ROMANO (1499?–1546)
Head and Hands of a Weeping Mother – fragment of a cartoon for 'The Massacre of the Innocents'
Brush and bodycolour on joined paper, 55.3 x 45.6cm
The Governing Body, Christ Church, Oxford

48 BARTOLOMMEO MONTAGNA (*c.* 1450-1523) *Bust of the Virgin*
Black chalk or charcoal, and stump, heightened with white chalk, 29 x 19.9cm
The Governing Body, Christ Church, Oxford

CATALOGUE

1 FEDERICO BAROCCI 1526-1612
Crucifixion
Charcoal and white chalk 51.4 x 40.6cm
The Syndics of the Fitzwilliam Museum, Cambridge

2 FEDERICO BAROCCI 1526-1612
Crucifixion
Pen and ink 20.3 x 17.5cm
The Syndics of the Fitzwilliam Museum, Cambridge

3 FRA BARTOLOMMEO (Baccio della Porta) 1472-1517
A Wooden Ravine
Pen and brown ink 23.7 x 31.3cm
Trustees of the British Museum

4 FRA BARTOLOMMEO (Baccio della Porta) 1472-1517
Five Nude Men
Pen and ink 15.7 x 18.6cm
Trustees of the British Museum

5 GEORG BASELITZ *b.* 1938
Study for Woodcut 1967
Pencil and blue chalk 61.1 x 43cm
Tate Gallery, Purchased 1984

6 MAX BECKMANN 1884-1950
Sheet of Sketchbook Drawings
Pencil 15.9 x 9.6cm
Trustees of the British Museum

7 UMBERTO BOCCIONI 1882-1916
Portrait Study for a Lost Sculpture
Pencil 33 x 24.4cm
The Syndics of the Fitzwilliam Museum, Cambridge

8 DAVID BOMBERG 1890-1957
Sappers at Work 1919 (ill. p.58)
Charcoal 67.5 x 56cm
The Trustees of the Imperial War Museum

9 LOUISE BOURGEOIS *b.* 1911
Untitled 1947
Ink and charcoal on paper 27.9 x 22.2cm
Karsten Schubert Ltd, London

10 PAUL BRIL 1554-1626
Landscape
Watercolour 20 x 27.3cm
The Syndics of the Fitzwilliam Museum, Cambridge

11 EDWARD BURRA 1905-76
Cabaret Scene 1930 (verso)
Pencil 61 x 48cm
Leeds City Art Galleries

12 LUCA CAMBIASO 1527-88
Dante and Virgil in the Infernal Regions
Pen and brown ink, brown wash, traces of black chalk
19.4 x 24.6cm
Courtauld Institute Galleries, London (Witt Collection)

13 LUCA CAMBIASO 1527-88
Noli me Tangere
Pen and brown ink, brown wash 36.3 x 24.6/24.8cm
Courtauld Institute Galleries, London (Witt Collection)

14 LUCA CAMBIASO 1527-88
The Crucifixion after 1570 (ill. p.59)
Pen, brown ink and wash 21.4 x 29.5cm
Whitworth Art Gallery, University of Manchester

15 ANTONIO CANALETTO 1697-1768
Venice: the South-West Angle of the Doge's Palace
Pen and brown ink over black chalk, some pricked indications
22.5 x 17.6cm
The Visitors of the Ashmolean Museum

16 AGOSTINO CARRACCI 1557-1602
Landscape, with Rest on the Flight into Egypt
Pen and brown ink 24 x 27.2cm
Courtauld Institute Galleries, London (Witt Collection)

17 AGOSTINO CARRACCI 1557-1602
Sheet of Studies with the Head of an Eagle and Men's Profiles and Caricatures (ill. p.37)
Pen and brown ink and some wash 14.6 x 20cm
Viscount Coke and the Trustees of the Holkham Estate

18 PAUL CEZANNE 1839-1906
Study from the Statuette of a Cupid c. 1890 (ill. p.60)
Black chalk 50.5 x 32.1cm
Trustees of the British Museum

19 SANDRO CHIA *b.* 1946
Seated Male Figure (ill. p.55)
Tempera and watercolour 25.4 x 20.3cm
The Syndics of the Fitzwilliam Museum, Cambridge

20 CIGOLI (Ludovico Cardi) 1559-1613
A Soldier on his Hands and Knees, Blowing
Black chalk (and some red chalk) heightened with bodycolour on
grey-blue paper 25 x 40.7cm
The Governing Body, Christ Church, Oxford

21 CLAUDE LORRAIN (Claude Gellée) 1600-82
Study of Sunlit Trees
Sepia wash over black chalk 21.2 x 31.2cm
Trustees of the British Museum

22 CLAUDE LORRAIN (Claude Gellée) 1600-82
Woodland Glade (ill. p.27)
Sepia wash over black chalk 20.5 x 27.2cm
Trustees of the British Museum

23 CLAUDE LORRAIN (Claude Gellée) 1600-82
View of the Belvedere and the Fortification of the Vatican
Pen and brown ink and wash 16 x 40.9cm
Viscount Coke and the Trustees of the Holkham Estate

24 CLAUDE LORRAIN (Claude Gellée) 1600-82
View of Genoa
Pen and brown ink and wash 21.1 x 32.5cm
Viscount Coke and the Trustees of the Holkham Estate

25 SUE COE *b.* 1951
American Exploits 1989
Ink and mixed media 34.3 x 22.9cm
Ivan Florence

26 JOHN SELL COTMAN 1782-1842
Domfront c. 1822
Pencil and wash 28.9 x 42.3cm
Leeds City Art Galleries

27 ALEXANDER COZENS 1717-86
Italian Landscape with Domed Building
Pencil and ink on prepared paper 10.2 x 16.2cm
Leeds City Art Galleries

28 ALEXANDER COZENS 1717-86
Study of a Tree
Watercolour on paper 15.9 x 19.7cm
Whitworth Art Gallery, University of Manchester

29 LORENZO DI CREDI *c.* 1458-1537
Head of a Boy in a Cap (ill. p.65)
Silverpoint, heightened with white 21.8 x 21.2cm
The Governing Body, Christ Church, Oxford

30 RICHARD DADD 1817-1887
Head of a Norseman
Pencil and watercolour 13.3 x 11.7cm
The Syndics of the Fitzwilliam Museum, Cambridge

31 HILAIRE-GERMAIN-EDGAR DEGAS 1834-1917
Elisabeth de Valois, after Moro c. 1889
Black chalk, charcoal and stump 41 x 27.6cm
The Syndics of the Fitzwilliam Museum, Cambridge

32 HILAIRE-GERMAIN-EDGAR DEGAS 1834-1917
Studies after Italian Madonnas
Pencil, with traces of red crayon 26.2 x 34cm
The Syndics of the Fitzwilliam Museum, Cambridge

33 ALBRECHT DÜRER 1471-1528
Head of the Dead Christ (cover ill.)
Charcoal 31 x 22.1cm
Trustees of the British Museum

34 ALBRECHT DÜRER 1471-1528
Study of Eve (ill. p.18)
Pen and brown ink and wash 27.8 x 17.1cm
Trustees of the British Museum

35 SIR ANTHONY VAN DYCK 1599-1641
Studies for a Virgin & Child with Saints
Pen and sepia and sepia wash 29.6 x 19.1cm
Trustees of the British Museum

36 SIR ANTHONY VAN DYCK 1599-1641
Study for the Lamentation (ill. p.21)
Black and white chalk 53.5 x 45cm
Trustees of the British Museum

37 SIR ANTHONY VAN DYCK 1599-1641
Study for St. Mary Magdalene
Black chalk and sepia wash 26 x 15.7cm
Trustees of the British Museum

38 ADAM ELSHEIMER 1578-1610
The Crucifixion
Pen and bistre with brush work in indian ink and bodycolour
12.1 x 10.3cm
The Visitors of the Ashmolean Museum

39 SIR JACOB EPSTEIN 1880-1959
Study of a Negress c. 1929
Pencil 43.2 x 34 cm
Leeds City Art Galleries

40 JOHN FLAXMAN 1755-1826
*Andromache Swooning at the Sight of Hector's Body being
Dragged Behind Achilles' Chariot*
Pencil 21.6 x 26cm
Sheffield City Art Galleries

41 JOHN FLAXMAN 1755-1826
Comfort the Afflicted
Pen and ink and watercolour 19.8 x 31.5cm
Whitworth Art Gallery, University of Manchester

42 JOHN FLAXMAN 1755-1826
To Whom Ye Yield Yourselves...
Pencil, pen and ink and watercolour 18 x 20.7cm
Whitworth Art Gallery, University of Manchester

43 FRANCIABIGIO (Francisco di Cristofano) 1482-1525
Head of a Young Man early 16th century (ill. p.63)
Black chalk with touches of white 25.1 x 20.6cm
The Board of Trustees of the Victoria & Albert Museum

44 HENRY FUSELI 1741-1825
Descent of Odin
Grey wash over pen and brown ink 26.9 x 37.6cm
Trustees of the British Museum

45 HENRY FUSELI 1741-1825
Hamlet at Ophelia's Grave
Grey wash over pen and brown ink 22.3 x 37.8cm
Trustees of the British Museum

46 HENRY FUSELI 1741-1825
The Kiss
Pencil 23.7 x 33.3cm
Trustees of the British Museum

47 SCHOOL OF GALLI-BIBIENA, 18th century
A Hall of State (ill. p.47)
Pen and brown ink, grey and pink wash 42.8 x 58cm
British Architectural Library Drawings Collection/Royal Institute
of British Architects

48 HENRI GAUDIER-BRZESKA 1891-1915
Standing Male Nude c. 1913
Pen and ink 48.3 x 36.8cm
Kettle's Yard, University of Cambridge

49 THEODORE GERICAULT 1791-1824
Centaur Abducting a Nymph
Pen and ink 23 x 17.2cm
Private Collection

50 THEODORE GERICAULT 1791-1824
Mameluke Horsemen in Battle
Pen and ink 19.7 x 27.9cm
Private Collection

51 MARK GERTLER 1892-1939
Seated Nude Figure 1923
Brown chalk 35.8 x 31.9cm
Leeds City Art Galleries

52 JACOB DE GHEYN II 1565-1629
A Witches' Sabbath
Pen and brown ink and grey wash, with some bodycolour on
buff paper 37.7 x 51.9cm
The Governing Body, Christ Church, Oxford

53 ALBERTO GIACOMETTI 1901-66
Portrait of the Artist's Brother 1948
Pencil 49 x 31cm
Robert and Lisa Sainsbury Collection, University of East Anglia

54 ERIC GILL 1882-1940
Study for a Female Nude 1927
Pencil and chalk 26.8 x 20.7cm
Leeds City Art Galleries

55 JAMES GILLRAY 1757-1815
Portrait of George Humphrey Jnr (ill. p.49)
Pen and ink 37 x 49.2cm
Trustees of the British Museum

56 PALMA GIOVANE (Giacomo Palma) 1544-1628
Two Heads in Profile (verso) Leaf from a sketchbook
Pen and brown ink 19 x 14.3cm
The Governing Body, Christ Church, Oxford

57 JULIO GONZALEZ 1876-1942
Stern Face 1936
Pen and watercolour 24.1 x 15.9cm
Tate Gallery, Presented by Mme Roberta Gonzalez-Richard,
the artist's niece 1972

58 FRANCISCO JOSE GOYA 1746-1828
Locos (ill. p.54)
Chalk 19.1 x 14.4cm
Trustees of the British Museum

59 EMILIO GRECO *b*. 1913
Head of a Girl 1954 (ill. p.39)
Pen and ink 49.8 x 35.6 cm
Tate Gallery, Purchased 1955

60 GEORGE GROSZ 1893-1959
Couple at the Table
Pen and brush 42.6 x 53.5cm
Trustees of the British Museum

61 FRANCESCO GUARDI 1712-93
Head and Shoulders of a Young Woman
Pen and ink 19.6 x 31.8cm
The Board of Trustees of the Victoria & Albert Museum

62 GUERCINO (Giovanni Francesco Barbieri) 1591-1666
A Woman Seized by Soldiers being Rescued by a Youth
Pen and brown ink and wash 27.6 x 37.7cm
Trustees of the British Museum

63 GUERCINO (Giovanni Francesco Barbieri) 1591-1666
Half-length Study of Cleopatra
Pen and brown ink 16.3 x 17.5cm
Trustees of the British Museum

64 GUERCINO (Giovanni Francesco Barbieri) 1591-1666
Hercules and the Hydra (ill. p.17)
Red chalk 21.1 x 31.1cm
Trustees of the British Museum

65 GUERCINO (Giovanni Francesco Barbieri) 1591-1666
Landscape with two Fishermen (ill. p.41)
Pen and brown ink 15.8 x 19cm
Trustees of the British Museum

66 ATTRIBUTED TO TOTOYA HOKKEI 1780-1850
Promenading Courtesan c. 1820
Brush and ink 27 x 18.7cm
Collection of Mr and Mrs Dennis Wiseman

67 HANS HOLBEIN THE ELDER *c*. 1460/65-1524
Head of a woman
Pen and bistre 10.2 x 13.5cm
Trustees of the British Museum

68 HANS HOLBEIN THE YOUNGER 1497/8-1543
Portrait of a Lady, Thought to be Anne Boleyn (ill. p.35)
Black chalk, partly stumped, and red chalk; brush and black ink,
yellow wash on pink prepared paper 32.1 x 23.5cm
Trustees of the British Museum

69 WOLFGANG HUBER *c*. 1480/90-1553
Landscape
Pen and indian ink 19 x 15.8cm
The Visitors of the Ashmolean Museum

70 INDIAN, ANONYMOUS, 19th century?
Tomb, Fatephur Sikri
Pen and ink and brown ink 48.5 x 66.5cm
British Architectural Library Drawings Collection/Royal Institute
of British Architects

71 JEAN-AUGUSTE-DOMINIQUE INGRES 1780-1867
Portrait of John, 7th Earl of Sandwich, as a Child 1816
Pencil 32.4 x 21cm
Private Collection

72 ISSHI BUNSHU 1608-45
Zen drawing of a contemplative figure c. 1640 (ill. p.30)
Brush and ink 27.1 x 18.6cm
Collection of Mr and Mrs Dennis Wiseman

73 JAIPURI SCHOOL
Portrait of Pratap Singh of Jaipur as Prince and Ruler
(reigned 1779-1803) (ill. p.34)
Chalk and ink with pointed brush, touched with white 57.5 x 71cm
Collection Howard Hodgkin, London

74 GWEN JOHN 1876-1939
Portrait of Winifred John 1939 (ill. p.64)
Pencil on buff paper (stamped with atelier mark) 15.9 x 15.9cm
Sheffield City Art Galleries

75 ANGELICA KAUFFMAN 1740-1807
The Letter: Half-length Figure Seated at a Table (ill. p.8)
Black chalk 11.1 x 12.3cm
Trustees of the British Museum

76 MATSUMURA KEIBUN 1779-1843
Bracken c. 1820 (ill. p.25)
Brush and ink 25.6 x 39.4 cm
Collection of Mr and Mrs Dennis Wiseman

77 ERNST KIRCHNER 1880-1938
Three Nudes 1920
Black crayon 45.5 x 31cm
Leicestershire Museums, Arts and Records Service

78 LEON KOSSOFF *b*. 1926
Drawing for 'Woman Ill in Bed Surrounded by Family' 1965 (ill. p.51)
Pen and ink 29.8 x 22.2cm
Tate Gallery, Presented by the artist 1981

79 KUNIYOSHI 1797-1861
Drawing for woodcut: Arashi Kichisaburo as a Wrestler
Pen, ink and brush 32.7 x 23.2cm
Sheffield City Art Galleries

80 FERNAND LEGER 1881-1955
Mother and Child 1922
Pencil on paper 40 x 30.5cm
Private Collection

81 ALPHONSE LEGROS 1837-1911
Portrait of Sir Arthur Strong
Silver point 29.5 x 23.8cm
The Syndics of the Fitzwilliam Museum, Cambridge

82 PERCY WYNDHAM LEWIS 1882-1957
Portrait of Miss E 1920 (ill. p.33)
Pencil 38 x 56cm
Manchester City Art Galleries

83 PERCY WYNDHAM LEWIS 1882-1957
Head of James Joyce 1921
Ink and watercolour 27.3 x 19.7cm
Sheffield City Art Galleries

84 SIR EDWARD LANDSEER LUTYENS 1869-1944
Triumphal Arch c. 1923 (ill. p.14)
Pen and ink and coloured chalk on letterhead 25.5 x 20cm
British Architectural Library Drawings Collection/Royal Institute
of British Architects

85 NICOLAES MAES 1634-93
A Milkseller at a House Door (ill. p.31)
Pen and wash 15.2 x 18.7cm
The Syndics of the Fitzwilliam Museum, Cambridge

86 ARISTIDE MAILLOL 1861-1944
Recumbent Nude Seen from Behind
Red chalk 22.9 x 32.4cm
The Syndics of the Fitzwilliam Museum, Cambridge

87 HENRI MATISSE 1869-1954
Visage 1951 (ill. p.29)
Brush & indian ink 43.5 x 33.5cm
Libby Howie and John Pillar Fine Art

88 HENRI MATISSE 1869-1954
Nude Female Torso 1947
Conté crayon ? 36.5 x 25cm
Private Collection

89 PAULA MODERSOHN-BECKER 1867-1907
Sketch of a Peasant Girl (ill. p.53)
Charcoal 18.7 x 22.5cm
The Board of Trustees of the Victoria & Albert Museum

90 AMEDEO MODIGLIANI 1884-1920
Portrait of a Woman (? Anna Zborowska) *c*. 1917
Pencil 46 x 29.5cm
Robert and Lisa Sainsbury Collection, University of East Anglia

91 BARTOLOMMEO MONTAGNA *c*. 1450-1523
Bust of the Virgin (ill. p.67)
Black chalk or charcoal, and stump, heightened with white chalk
29 x 19.9cm
The Governing Body, Christ Church, Oxford

92 PAUL NASH 1889-1946
Nightfall, Zillebeke District 1917
Pen and pastel on brown paper 25.7 x 35.6cm
The Trustees of the Imperial War Museum

93 CHRISTOPHER RICHARD WYNNE NEVINSON 1889-1946
Study for 'Returning to the Trenches' 1914-15
Charcoal 14.6 x 20.6cm
Tate Gallery, Purchased 1959

94 VICTOR NEWSOME *b*. 1935
Profile Head 1982 (ill. p.57)
Pencil; grey wash, heightened with acrylic white, squared in pencil
32.8 x 46cm
Trustees of the British Museum

95 ISACK VAN OSTADE 1621-49
A Reeling Drunkard, Brandishing a Tankard
Pen, brown ink and wash 15.5 x 8.1cm
Courtauld Institute Galleries, London (Witt Collection)

96 SAMUEL PALMER 1805-81
The Sleeping Shepherd 1826-1832
Pen, ink and watercolour 15.7 x 18.8cm
Whitworth Art Gallery, University of Manchester

97 BERNARDO PARENTINO 1437-1531
An Allegory, in Imitation of an Antique Relief (ill. p.19)
Pen and brown ink, on vellum 29.5 x 21.4cm
The Governing Body, Christ Church, Oxford

98 (School of) BARTOLOMMEO PASSAROTTI 1529-92
Study for a Prophet
Brown ink 38.4 x 24.4cm
The Syndics of the Fitzwilliam Museum, Cambridge

99 PABLO PICASSO 1881-1973
Seated Figure
Pen and brown ink 30.5 x 22.5cm
The Visitors of the Ashmolean Museum

100 PABLO PICASSO 1881-1973
Goat's Skull *c*. 1951
Pen and ink with wash 50.6 x 65.4cm
Birmingham City Museums and Art Gallery

101 PABLO PICASSO 1881-1973
The Kiss 1967
Pencil 50.5 x 64.5cm
Private Collection

102 GIOVANNI BATTISTA PIRANESI 1720-78
Studies of Figures and of Anatomical Details
Reed pen and red chalk 19.5 x 27.1cm
The Visitors of the Ashmolean Museum

103 GIOVANNI BATTISTA PIRANESI 1720-78
The Pantheon in an Imaginary Architectural Setting
Pen and dark brown ink and grey brown wash over some
black chalk 11.9 x 17.5cm
Courtauld Institute Galleries, London (Witt Collection)

104 AFTER NICOLAS POUSSIN 1593/4-1665
Centaur Studies
Pen and bistre 18.3 x 18.9cm
Trustees of the British Museum

105 PIERRE PUVIS DE CHAVANNES 1824-98
Study for the sketch for the 'Ludus Pro Patria'
Charcoal and chalk 21.9 x 19.4cm
The Syndics of the Fitzwilliam Museum, Cambridge

106 MARKUS RAETZ *b*. 1941
Untitled, Carona 1973
Red, yellow, blue and black inks on 3 sheets of paper, each 49.3 x
69cm, mounted vertically on cheesecloth 156 x 76.6 x 4.5cm
Tate Gallery, Purchased 1987

107 RAJASTHAN, SAWAR SCHOOL
Page of Sketches *c*. 1700 (ill. p.23)
Brush drawing 40.6 x 62.9cm
Collection Howard Hodgkin, London

108 PAULA REGO *b*. 1935
Study for 'The Nanny' 1990
Pen and brown ink and wash 25 x 20cm
Collection of the Artist

109 REMBRANDT HARMENSZ VAN RIJN 1606-69
Landscape with a Man Sitting on a Sluice Gate (ill. p.10)
Reed pen and ink 14.6 x 25.4cm
The Board of Trustees of the Victoria & Albert Museum

110 REMBRANDT HARMENSZ VAN RIJN 1606-69
View over Flat Country with Amsterdam in the Distance
Pen and bistre and wash 7.8 x 21cm
The Board of Trustees of the Victoria & Albert Museum

111 DIEGO RIVERA 1886-1957
Portrait of Robert Tannahill 1932
Red chalk 73.6 x 57.8cm
Birmingham City Museums and Art Gallery

112 WILLIAM ROBERTS 1895-1980
Drawing for 'The Return of Ulysses' 1913
Pen and chalk 30.5 x 46cm
Tate Gallery, Purchased 1972

113 STUDIO OF GIULIO ROMANO (Giulio Pippi) 1499?-1546
Head and Hands of a Weeping Mother - fragment of a cartoon for
The Massacre of the Innocents (ill. p.66)
Brush and bodycolour on joined paper 55.3 x 45.6cm
The Governing Body, Christ Church, Oxford

114 GEORGE ROMNEY 1734-1802
The Birth of Man *c*. 1793
Pencil 11.4 x 15.6cm
The Syndics of the Fitzwilliam Museum, Cambridge

115 GEORGE ROMNEY 1734-1802
Gladiator on Horseback
Pen with brown ink and brown wash over pencil 32.4 x 37.1cm
The Syndics of the Fitzwilliam Museum, Cambridge

116 GEORGE ROMNEY 1734-1802
A Shepherd Boy Asleep Watched by his Dog at The Approach of a
Thunderstorm (ill. p.16)
Grey watercolour wash over black chalk 27.1 x 30cm
The Syndics of the Fitzwilliam Museum, Cambridge

117 GEORGE ROMNEY 1734-1802
Two Young Girls Talking (ill. p.28)
Brush with dark brown watercolour wash over pencil 34.3 x 21cm
The Syndics of the Fitzwilliam Museum, Cambridge

118 SALVATOR ROSA 1615-73
Man Suspended from his Arms
Pen and brown ink and wash 16.3 x 8cm
Viscount Coke and the Trustees of the Holkham Estate

119 GEORGE ROMNEY 1734-1802
Fragment of Classical Architecture in Landscape
Pen and ink 17.8 x 16.5cm
The Syndics of the Fitzwilliam Museum, Cambridge

120 DANTE GABRIEL ROSSETTI 1828-82
Rossetti Sitting to Miss Siddal 1853
Pen and sepia ink on writing paper, shaded with finger 13 x 17.6cm
Birmingham City Museums and Art Gallery

121 FOLLOWER OF PETER PAUL RUBENS
Study of a Nude Man Tormented by Demons
Black chalk, heightened with white, and indian ink and bistre on a slightly yellowed paper 37.9 x 24cm
The Visitors of the Ashmolean Museum

122 PETER PAUL RUBENS 1577-1640
Abel Slain by Cain (ill. p.21)
Red chalk 20.6 x 21.6cm
The Syndics of the Fitzwilliam Museum, Cambridge

123 FRANCESCO SALVIATI 1510-53
Portrait of a Youth, Head and Shoulders, Full-face
Black chalk 27 x 21.6cm
The Board of Trustees of the Victoria & Albert Museum

124 ANDRE DUNOYER DE SEGONZAC
A Soldier 1917
Pen and wash 19.2 x 12.3cm
Robert and Lisa Sainsbury Collection, University of East Anglia

125 WALTER SICKERT 1860-1942
He Killed his Father in a Fight (ill. p.50)
Pencil 38.4 x 28.3cm
Whitworth Art Gallery, University of Manchester

126 LUCA SIGNORELLI 1441?-1523
Sleeping Youth
Chalk 15.6 x 30.8cm
Trustees of the British Museum

127 ELISABETTA SIRANI 1638-65
Head of the Virgin with a Halo of Stars (ill. p.38)
Black chalk (with corrections in white chalk) on joined paper (cartoon) 47.2 x 36.8cm
The Governing Body, Christ Church, Oxford

128 SIR STANLEY SPENCER 1891-1959
Interior View of a Ship 1940
Pencil 42.3 x 53.3cm
The Trustees of the Imperial War Museum

129 SIR STANLEY SPENCER 1891-1959
Decorative Composition (Study for the Leeds Decoration) c. 1920
Pencil and wash 50.2 x 34.9cm
Leeds City Art Galleries

130 TALPINO (Enea Salmeggia) c. 1565?-1626
Proportion Studies
Pen and brown ink, some black chalk 24.6 x 17.3cm
The Governing Body, Christ Church, Oxford

131 AGOSTINO TASSI c. 1580-1644
Landscape after Elsheimer
Pen and wash 18.6 x 25.9cm
The Syndics of the Fitzwilliam Museum, Cambridge

132 GIOVANNI BATTISTA TIEPOLO 1696-1770
Drawing of Farm Buildings (ill. p.45)
Pen and bistre 17 x 28.2cm
Trustees of the British Museum

133 GIOVANNI BATTISTA TIEPOLO 1696-1770
Oil Sketch of a Head (ill. p.11)
Watercolours 36 x 28.3cm
Trustees of the British Museum

134 GIOVANNI DOMENICO TIEPOLO 1727-1804
Pulcinella on a Satyr
Pen and ink and brown wash 29.5 x 41.2cm
Trustees of the British Museum

135 DOMENICO TINTORETTO 1560-1635
The Martyrdom of St. Stephen
Monochrome oils on blue paper 34.5 x 18.7cm
The Governing Body, Christ Church, Oxford

136 JACOPO TINTORETTO 1518-94
Christ on the Cross (ill. p.61)
Black chalk heightened with white on grey paper, squared in black chalk 38.7 x 26.7cm
The Board of Trustees of the Victoria & Albert Museum

137 STUDIO OF JACOPO TINTORETTO
Studies of Antique Sculpture (verso) (ill. p.15)
Charcoal, touched with white bodycolour on blue paper 41.7 x 28cm
The Governing Body, Christ Church, Oxford

138 CARLO URBINO (da Crema) Working 2nd half of 16th century
Study for a Painting
Watercolour 23.3 x 21.6cm
The Syndics of the Fitzwilliam Museum, Cambridge

139 THOMAS VAUGHAN 1836-74
Study in Sciography 1857 (ill. p.6)
Pen and wash 44.7 x 64.5cm
British Architectural Library Drawings Collection/Royal Institute of British Architects

140 DANIELE (RICCIARELLI) DA VOLTERRA 1509-66
A Young Woman Asleep
Pen and brown ink with brown wash 13.3 x 8.3cm
The Visitors of the Ashmolean Museum

141 EDWARD WADSWORTH 1889-1949
Granite Quarries 1919 (ill. p.43)
Pen and ink 25.3 x 36.7cm
Whitworth Art Gallery, University of Manchester

142 JEAN-ANTOINE WATTEAU 1684-1721
Back of a Female Figure (ill. p.42)
Red chalk 13.7 x 7.9cm
The Syndics of the Fitzwilliam Museum, Cambridge

143 FEDERICO ZUCCARO 1542-1609
Composition of Three Male Figures
Pen and brown wash over black chalk 29.1 x 22.4cm
The Visitors of the Ashmolean Museum

144 FEDERICO ZUCCARO 1542-1609
A Man Drawing by Moonlight from the Window of a House (ill. p.46)
Pen, brown ink and brown wash 35.6 x 17.8cm
The Visitors of the Ashmolean Museum